MURMURINGS – A COLLECTION

Books by Don Davison

An Outline of a Philosophy of the Consciousness of Truth
The Concept of Personhood in the Evolutionary Process of Being
The Game of Life: A Player's Manual for Executives and Others
Sign Posts: A Collection of Essays, Vol. I
Sign Posts: A Collection of Essays, Vol. II
Sign Posts: A Collection of Essays, Vol. III

Poetry

Thoughts and Feelings Book I
Thoughts and Feelings Book II
Needles from the Ponderosas at Zirahuen
Seeds from the Ponderosas at Zirahuen
Pitch from the Ponderosas at Zirahuen
Humus from the Ponderosas at Zirahuen
Sawdust from the Ponderosas at Zirahuen
Sun's rays through the Ponderosas at Zirahuen
Shadows beneath the Ponderosas at Zirahuen
Cones from the Ponderosas at Zirahuen
Pollen sifting from the Ponderosas at Zirahuen
Reflections from Lucerne
Searching Swamps
Questions
Time's Echoes
Memories

Collections

Always Extolling
Iris and Other Things
Pieces of the Journey
Through the Swamps of Time

Zirahuen
Phoenix, AZ
pathtotheself.com
DrDavison@pathtotheself.com

ISBN 978-0-9774039-2-9

Cover photo by Peter Davison (Lake Lucerne, Forest County, Wisconsin)
Author photo by Patricia Davison

A special thanks to Louella Holter and Ron Redsteer formerly of the Bilby
Research Center of Northern Arizona University for their editing and
illustration services, and to Tina Rosio, from W.

MURMURINGS – A COLLECTION

Don Davison

All of Don Davison's books have water on their covers. Water is one of the most essential attributes of the planet Earth; without it, life as we know it would not exist. It deserves our most considered attention.

Davison's collections of poetry all end with "Finding Pieces." Many of you have asked, where did the rules for the Game of Life come from? They come from many places and different times. Good hunting!

CONTENTS

To my parents –
Dave and Frances Davison.
They gave so much.

"Hawker of wares, what sell you but words?"
"Melodies of soul," I say.

THE FIRE OF LIFE

A fire reminds me of life –
it starts with a rush, then slows down,
and finally
begins to enjoy itself.

FLASHES

The place, the attitudes of time, the dryness,
the wetness, the heat, the cold,
the passage of creatures,
the wearing of the elements,
the permanence of change,
hidden holes, hallowed hollows
all filled with life's pregnant purpose.
Is the silver of the cloud diminished,
is the brilliance of the blue tarnished,
is the gold of the moon any less –
if one walks through life with problems?
They are all that they are –
magnificent in their every hue.
I believe in me and I believe in you.
There is a morality in carrying one's dreams
into others' arenas.
One must choose not to burden
anyone with their dreams.
To sit at the edge of a meadow and appreciate
all of the incredible events that go unnoticed
and unobserved by the bustling world
is to sense the silent peace of God
as He spends His moments laughing.
The right place,
the right time,
the right thing,
the right way …
Does the fiddler know for whom the bow is moved,
or seeking self does he play with that abandon
that gives him access to the All of Alls?

WHO AM I?

The roar of the jet cannot penetrate the silence of the moment.
Life is everything!
In one square meter of ground
there is more life than in an entire city.
Life is oh so grand,
and yet, where oh where my stand?
Where fresh water meets the salty seas –
the smell of thee and me.
Rotting grabs ...
life's giving moments.
A row of seagulls stand guarding the shore.
Tell me, who is chairman of the board?
The flow of the rivers, pushed and pulled,
tells me of the omnipresence of the Force.
To turn our vital essence to the wind
is to travel life's path with the spirit of humankind.

TO WAIT

The silent stillness presses home a presence that says,
"Waiting can be a delightful pastime."
Is not the birth of a blade of grass a precious
moment in the eternal process?
May we, as we are subject to the movement of the clock,
dispose a sensitivity that anticipates the knock?
What purpose does a shadow have that creeps across the day,
if not to enlighten in some way
all the things we hope and pray?

MY BARN

May my barn have snow some day hanging on the roof.
May I, standing in its shelter,
reflect while cleaning my horse's hoof,
that hay, wind, and sky were meant to be appreciated
from barn doors open to the season.
Will it be that being there
will bring me closer to that razor's edge of reason?
I think of summer fun and of some day
when hours will be spent just dreaming in the hay.
May my barn have snow some day
and may I lie there in the hay
passing moments with time to pray.

ROUGH EDGES

Fingers are led to needles, to leaves, and to bark.
They follow through to stumps, posts, and knots,
trailing ridges in the skeletons of life's remains.
Rough edges, do they give us those stark remembrances
of life's relentless push?
I think so and I love them for their presences
and staying shadows.
They stand against time and set
Faith, Hope, and Charity
in eternal form.

INSISTENCE AND TRUTH

"But Dad, how do you know?"
There are ways.
"But how can you tell how much they care?"
See those rose bushes?
"Yes, but what does that tell you?"
Notice the size of the gnarled old roots?
"Yes?"
Therein lies the secret of the care
that has given birth to many summers of beauty.

QUESTIONS

"But why, Daddy, did the grasshopper die?"
Because of the truck, the foot, the position, the circumstance …
A convoluted explanation and yet …
"But why, Daddy, did the grasshopper die?"
The Divine Plan unfolds in mysterious ways.
It is not for us to understand the whole.
But know this my son –
there is another grasshopper.
As the tiny head turns towards the future and its moments,
a small, telltale glint still holds,
"But why did the grasshopper die?"

THE GAME

I ask again in seeking, just what is my role?
The answer manifests in its simplicity where it's from.
Genus and species I know not,
but that the tiny creature would trouble itself
to cross home plate in the third inning
of my son's baseball game,
while I …
caught up in wonderings and cooperative effort,
stood tenaciously behind the catcher, umpiring his every effort.
In that simple display of grandeur,
a reflective mood was struck,
and I was reminded of the beauty of the All.
A calmness came over me as I concentrated on my task,
"Strike three, you're out!"
Was the final call.

FORGOTTEN SPOTS

Corners of dust,
curbs and gutters,
burned and soaked
in never seen space.
Dry, dead powder,
a pasty nuisance to the eyes,
nothing to the nose.
What purpose?
What value?
Then …
it's caught by swirling winds,
lofted to currents,
and carried away to be
laid in other places
to become blessed nutrients for the rose.

ARE WE ...

Are we all part of the last wave of independence,
cresting, rolling away from ourselves
just before we implode into the heart of the whole?
Is there enough strength of being
for us to be real
before we move off this present course?
Hush the wind,
still the ignorance of desire,
and let us see
the Truth.

CHANGE

Will there be some who will find
the "Mancha" of their origins?
There is not much that distills from
the history of human effort.
Most of the pulp of the day fades into humus.
But –
there are those pristine moments when
a soul shines throughout the ages.
Thank you, Heraclitus!
The winds blow – the waters rise.

LOS CREPUSCULOS DEL ANOCHECER*

The intensity of the day wanes,
a freedom of silence emerges.
Colors fade to one and then
the Oneness of the whole invites the one of the many
to journey forth from being bound by the "Others."
Expiation reigns!
It's a soft time
when Indistinct says,
"One is all there is!"
Simple silver and gold fragments
scatter in the heavens
and tranquility is questioned.
Some burn with an intensity,
others flash and twinkle in the void.
Ambivalence creeps into wonder.
Is our answer an emanation?
The Yin and Yang,
breathing in and exhaling.
It All says, "Yes!"
And then,
it All says, "No!"
The Yes feeds Hope,
the No feeds Faith,
and Charity offers the footpath to Eternity.

*Dusking twilight

THE WHY OF THE WHO AND THE WHAT

Can we, in some subtle way, do something
that they can see and understand?
Or, must we scream so that those living can appreciate
the serenity of the Eternal Flow?
From deep pain, hopeless prayers
are thrown into flames and lost in flight.
The truth is too quick to hold and own.
Time is not diseased,
movement is!
Want spills from the fire's glow.
It fills us and a thought is born.
It leaves us and a thought is dead.
The smell of smoke revives a palette of dreams and visions
of endless migrations from cave to cave
to the threshold of the present.
A fire truly is
a conflagration of tongues
that speak!

ONENESS

All roads are not without hills.
As we move forward in accumulating information,
statistics give us an opportunity to "predict patterns."
We must begin to own a greater picture of the truth.
Not just stripping and stealing from the whole,
we must recognize the integrity of each part.
When our forefathers spoke of "certain inalienable rights"
they did not have the current understanding of biology.
They were, however, grasping through philosophy
the threshold of sociology.
Today we mingle in the wake of sociobiology.
So that those living can appreciate
the serenity of the Eternal Flow,
we drag our treasures on steel rails
and we pull them over macadam.
We shuffle our feet as we stand in the cold winds of time.
The whole swirls relentlessly around us,
nomadic wanderers
who have lost the peace of presence.
Where are the keys?
Lost in the sand?
Squatting on our haunches or with our back to a tree,
staring into a fire reflecting on the patterns of the effervescent
is something we all need to do.
I wonder where I came from – Scotland and the hills?
Onwards, towards the savannahs and their edges,
to new worlds and their mountains!
Where will my sons and daughter go,
and their sons and daughters?

Will the evolutive effort be compassionate?
Perhaps, indiscriminately compassionate,
in that there is an abundance of all things.
That is, an abundance of life.
Dasien is! Dasien moves! Dasien cares!
The ONE, the COMPASSIONATE, the BEING
with all things as they come into being,
as they pass out of being,
as we touch them,
as they fade from us.
Embracing in that moment of holding
the HOLY TIME when choice is one!

TOO FAR?

So …
if the mountain top is too far away
can we lose our focus?
That is,
what are we doing in the present with and to ourselves?
A reflective mood must have some circumspection in the near.
There must be some existential imperative.

THE DEMOCRACY OF TRUTH

She struck a pose like a little gymnast, leaning back,
her tiny female form arching with arms outstretched,
"sticking" the perfect ten and screaming in delight,
"Peter Piper! Peter Piper! Pizza! Pizza!"
The scene took place in a super-affluent neighborhood
where the little shin-protected soccer player
had just returned home from "her game."
And the family,
who had dutifully attended "the game,"
were two harried professionals
in need of sustenance
– at any cost –
for themselves as well as their children.
So ... whatever!
Freedom of choice dictated by circumstance!
God bless the children!

REBAR

The deep hole in the ground, its edges gnawed,
was to be the permanent home for
"the footings"!
In the various angled corners bent figures of squatting men
twisted wire around blue-black uprights.
A latticework of intricate beauty
laced the entire belly of the hole.
Modern art, a skeleton, a patchwork quilt,
only the beholder's imagination would stifle the limits
of appreciation.
From dawn to dusk they labored in the hole,
accompanied by beads of dripping perspiration
and the ever-present din of machines
belching black and white smoke.
Festooned with helmets, bright orange vests, and gloves,
they must be important people.
And the truckloads of long black rods keep coming!
The artwork must be some important piece,
there is so much of it,
and the hole is, oh so deep!
Finally, tired workers leave the site and wend their way home.
There, they are greeted with barrages of childish questions.
"What did you do today, Daddy?"
Well, I'll tell you, I was very busy leaving telltale tracks
of a person's presence in history!
"Wow! That must sure be something to see.
Can we see them sometime, Daddy, please?"
Now that would be hard to do.
"Why, Daddy? Why?"

Well, those tracks are a gift to posterity.
Only future archaeologists may have a chance to see them.
"Oh? Where are they, then?"
Deep in the heart of the earth.
"Why did you do so much work that no one,
well hardly anyone, will ever see?"
To hold straight and fast all those tall buildings
that everyone will see.

LIGHT

The journey of light to me:
Fading black softness to golden dawn,
losing the day's brilliance to the dropping of the sun,
to the sap-soaked torch's smoky orange,
to the candle's hollow blue and yellow-white crown,
to the wick's steady flow,
to the incandescent's yellow buff,
to the fluorescent's insipidness,
to the eerie green presence of TV,
to the byways and highways
of the mercury vapor's intrusive pale,
to the soft, dying embers.
I prefer the fire's soft red glow.

LIFE

The taste of an apple,
a scene from a small cabin window,
a glen with an orchard
sloping gently to banks.
Dark water meandering through forests.
Ice crystals settling on tattered, curled leaves.
Those last green blades of meadow grass
hanging limp in the cold.
Steaming forms with winter's coats
standing in lean-to stalls.
The barn battened to the weather.
Black lines of fences,
gates left open
to roam and to shelter.
Warmth from the fire,
soft light from the day,
music bathing the soul.
The smells and sounds of kitchen labors,
murmurings of children,
the soft form of loyalty lying at foot.
With pen in hand and heart left still,
ideas come forth:
projects for the Christmas season,
projects for summer's heat,
thoughts of history's capricious tale,
sentiments of life's brief moment.

EATING

A calorie – then and now.

* * *

A scent taken in,
sent on a subtle breeze
to taunt and to tease.
Squatting near a fire,
stoking,
standing,
pacing,
anticipatory,
deepening the aromas of smoke and memories.
It will be so good.
Enraptured with the surroundings,
plans for the morrow,
sorting out the day's dreams and fears.
Mirrors of a sequined soul
reflecting the fullness of the great outdoors.
Food consumed,
mastication slowly done,
at the edge of the brook,
utensils rinsed and washed in the sand.
A whippoorwill's sharing.
Thank you, whoever and whatever you are.

* * *

Hurry!
Zapped by waves,
stuffed with heat in seconds.
Aseptic chambers where scents are consumed by some fan,
then rushed to a TV tray.
Bolted between commercials,
paced by the scenes on the screen.
Where was that calorie?
Was it needed?
Was it used?
Did I miss or forget something?

A THOUGHT

How much does it weigh?
Where does it sit?
Does it have a life of its own?
Just what do the mystics mean when they say –
"ONE?"
Is there some magnificent formula that holds all the answers?
Is there an eternal and infinite focus that belongs to a thought?
Or, are they so discrete that they belong to themselves?
How does one know what a remnant of one is?
What could it possibly be?
How big is a thought?
Does it matter upon what the thought lies?
Is an evil thought a condemnation to eternal punishment?
Is a blessed one a guarantee of eternal bliss?
Is the Beatific Vision that "Right Thought"?
Does the Great One give us that final opportunity to choose?
How can we think of the One?
Is It a flat face, all there now,
or is It a moving thing?
How could It be simply there, if One is everything?
Which thought to choose?

The task is not an easy one
among the many that are so beautiful.
Would just any do?
Yes, because they all lead to It.
Then, is there a Hell?
Not ultimately –
but one could wander for an awfully long time
among the many thoughts
before coming home to rest.
And still I ask,
What is a thought?
Are they really alive?
Do they "really" have a life of their own?

HANGING THE LEATHER

The harness, hames and collar,
singletree and chain,
all hung to rest.
Who cut the leather,
did the stitching, set the rivets?
When did black creep into brown and seal edges?
Smooth and pliable, coiled and supple,
hanging, hugging, all just right.
One thing we know,
it wasn't made for Diamond,
but he wore it with a sanctioned pride,
or was it that he just wore it
and the pride business was mine?
Not quite,
from hidden pockets to landings
he heaved his might to left and right
missing stumps, rocks, and roots,
a biodance of great proportions.
The day's labor finished at the creek,
muzzle sipping from a black mirror.
Great droughts taken.
Majestic head lifted and shaken.
Droplets leaving sagging lips.

And then …
a soft thud as leather, chain and wood meet
the evening's resting place.
Steam rising in the dim light of the barn's corner.
Leather wet with sweat and scent,
slippery to the arm and hand,
warm with heat from heaving sides.
Never heavy at day's end,
just well done.
Grain poured out.
Bails broken.
A repast for beast and friend set forth.
Munching mixed with heavy breathing.
Thoughts …
Time working with a sentient thing,
conversations of one word full of simple truths,
all of which get something done.
Just another day at Timber Ranch with Diamond.

THE SONG OF THE AXE

Memories of crisp winter air,
the singing of the metal,
the cadence of a song.
Whose back and arms were swinging
with feet placed upon the logs among the leaves and bracken,
or buried in the snow?
What was at hand that demanded the movement?
Who played?
What magnificent instrument was he using?
Firewood for winter evenings,
logs for some far-off mill,
veneer, that precious new commodity,
for furniture or packaging,
whatever!
The real truth was that the axe sang "to make a living,"
to do something that gave us some return.
And also because we loved swinging it,
we loved dancing in the forest,
becoming one with the arc of the axe.
Hitting the branch at just the right angle.
Attacking the larger ones with just enough blows.
Knowing the notes and the playing of tunes,
and so the axe sang.
It sang through spring and summer –
the Aspen Season.

It sang through fall –
the Bucking Up
and Firewood Season.
Then it sang though winter.
To each season there was a special ring.
Wood is soft and gentle,
wood is hard and brittle,
and sometimes just plain frozen,
but even then it still has a tone all its own.
We worked and it sang and we listened to its song.
In the early morning dawn,
in the heat of the day,
in the waning moments of the afternoon,
amidst the rumblings of far-off storms,
in the silence of the green,
we listened as hearts wondered into life.
The song of the axe,
a piece of poetry lost to changing times,
but I remember a time when the song of the axe
graced the woodlands with soaring hearts,
sending branches to the forest floor.

THE FOUR-WAY STOP

"What happened at the corner?
Something is missing."
The Stop Light blinks its incessant tricolor message.
The Stop Lights have come to give us greater freedom.
"Freedom from what?"

* * *

I reflect –
I remember a time not so long ago when ...

* * *

From those many opportunities along the trail,
pulling over,
waving,
helping others,
moving on towards our individual destiny
in a land so large we could help
our fellow travelers and neighbors
and still know we would get to where we were going
in plenty of time.
A four-way stop where we could witness
the character of a nation:
a tip of the hat,
a wave of the hand,
a nod of the head,
a pause ...
A vast array of cues and gestures
passing gently from the heart
as we "gave way" to others,
and friends we recognized.

When towns are small enough to have four-way stops
they also have familiar faces.
New drivers in their tentative peering,
older folks with their on-purpose poses,
lovers stealing kisses,
mothers adjusting little bodies,
children making faces to the rear.
A host of images flash before me and I know they are gone.
Gone forever.

* * *

"Why are you letting them go first?"
Well, some because they got there first and …
some because we have an opportunity to practice
being an American –
to practice being neighborly.
It's just a way of sharing the road.
You see, son, we are all pioneers of sorts.
You never know where a person is off to or coming from,
so when you can it's a nice gesture to wave them on,
especially the young ones who are sometimes in such a hurry.
"Why, Dad?"
Because they forget to look sometimes and because –
if we make it a sweeping gesture
they will acknowledge and remember,
and when they grow up they will then
share the road with others.
"Can I help?"
Sure, son.

And so we always asked each other
as we approached the crossroads.
We soon got to be such a good team that we would just
look at each other and make our move,
usually just a slight nod and a gentle movement of the hand.

* * *

And then the lights went up and ...

* * *

He was saying,
"Where will we go to see our friends?
Where will we go to see so many people and be so kind?
Where will we go to practice being an American?"
Through misty eyes I whispered,
I don't know, son, we'll have to find someplace, won't we?

METAL AND WOOD

Rolling stock,
dreams moving across a continent,
carried on metal rims sweated onto wooden wheels.
Hubs set with spokes of oak and ash.
Huge, cumbersome, heavy and homey,
they were the landships of their day.
Conestogas,
freights,
whatever it took to get them there.
Boards cut and bolted,
metal straps bent to angles,
soon to rust and yet to hold.
All to be recycled at journey's end.
Some new and off the wagonwright's lot,
with new wheels from a wheelwright's bench.
Some old from the Cumberland Trail,
some from the Northwest Territory,
all filled with people.
Some with fears,
some with dreams,
all moving west.
Slivers stuck in hands from their new or worn sides
when gripped, as trouble from the rugged trail
or "others" came their way.
Dust gathered from the scraping and the jostling
as things rode along the trail,
wearing odd designs in cross-grain patterns
on the sides and floors.

The weight of necessary treasures
brought from home for need or heart,
all adding to the mosaic of the cargo's tracks.
On top of the load were bedrolls
where families slept,
where children traced with short little fingers
the patterns of the wood,
where late-night embraces of tired bodies produced new life.
Then came the rain to raise the grain,
the mud to add grit,
and the rolling, rocking movement of the wagon
to give destiny to it all.
Brown and black scorched patterns on the canvas
told stories of forgotten evenings
when a soft yellow glow gave warmth
and enveloped the huddled life within,
providing just enough light for a verse or two from
the Good Book.
A canopy for a huge desert schooner
protected wandering souls from heat, wind, and the dark,
when love was shared and
fatigue left chores undone.
Sweat-stained boards where disease and fear
spent silent hours, when terror baked the body,
leaving a crystalline film of salt behind
for a future meal to be mined by a porcupine.
And all of this was only to the inside –
the outside is another story altogether.
Beaten and battered by all manner of things,
from weather with its careless compass
and its four apocalyptic horsemen:

Wind with sand polishing the surface,
sun with heat drying and bleaching essence and color,
rain graying the boards,
and frost leading to snow
that split from tiny pockets, splinters from the planks.
Then there were those other rattling, shifting denizens,
External Cargo!
Lashed on for easy access or lack of space and
those waiting points and edges that the trail
presented as branches,
stubs, and rocks.
All to scar the skin.
Knife marks as they were placed at rest from work.
Axe tracks as edges scraped their resting places
and not a few with thin slits from arrowheads,
or holes from some muzzle where lead lay buried.
Then there was the grease
from hands and hubs as quick stops were made
and a body was again hauled up to that worn seat
where sat aching backsides and when a pillow was not enough,
a walk along the trail with a hand on the edge of the wagon
was all that one looked forward to.
A tailgate with scents of nourishment,
stains of sage hen and deer,
where spilled flour mixed with dust
and biscuits were rolled out.
Where fruit pies sat and cooled
when berries were discovered along the way.
New sights and sounds at every turn,
nothing was familiar.
The great landscape of God's handiwork,
assessed at every hour with hoping heart and weary body.

Wonder fed dreams of perfect little valleys where rivers
meandered in lazy curves and death and hardship
were long forgotten –
until our eyes fell upon
that door,
that headboard,
that porch swing or bench,
a hinge,
a hub,
a hoop,
all bits and pieces of that grand old wagon.
Tears welled and fell again for those we left along the way,
fell for those whose dreams helped us believe in ours,
and for those who bought their dream at the final hour
for the ultimate price.
A scattered relic's power provides
a time of reflection and prayer
for those who helped us move across a continent
and never saw those valleys and meandering streams
with little homes dotting the banks,
or heard the fiddle and the salutations
and in the background the laughter
of playing children.
New homes and new towns,
new streets and new neighborhoods,
all chapters of a nation's history
written by intrepid souls
who put everything in a wagon
and left in search of a dream.

THE VOICE

A scream, shout, whisper, prayer
all moments of the human voice.
Ah, but there are so many more.
The soft babblings of children.
The shrieks of delight in play.
The murmurings of friendly conversation.
Commands barked to troops or workers.
The roar of the stadium crowd,
a host of variations.
And yet –
we wait upon the word.
It tells us so much about so many –
including ourselves.
The vibrant "Canto Yo" of the species,
that articulation giving sound and meaning.
They tell us that it's only about 15–20 percent
of our communication repertoire.
A symphony of effort produces such cacophony of sounds.
We seem to be all words.
Asked to paint our feelings
we lapse into language.
We attempt some intimate interchange
and syntax is the outcome.

The voice takes an inordinate position on the stage
and we sing …
an aria,
a gregorian,
a ballad,
a folk piece,
a popular tune,
a holy chant.
Or we speak …
a lecture,
condolences,
a mass,
a political rally,
a bar mitzvah,
a thank you to our God.
And finally –
a "good night, I love you,"
says it all.

THE CORNER POSTS

A stark, jagged interruption stands against the elements,
just a fence post most would say.
But not for me,
for me it's a way of life.
A life of purpose,
a statement that says something to the world.
I learned at an early age to circumscribe "the Ranch"
in the spring and in the fall.
There was a ritual connected with those hikes.
We would come up to a place and Dad would say,
"Can you find it?"
In the early going it was difficult.
We thought there would be some monument of sorts,
after all this was *our* land.
That wasn't the case.
He left things pretty much just the way he found them,
a metal post so rusty that it looked like an old branch
protruding from the humus.
Some were old wooden stakes,
weathered and surrounded by a few rocks –
those glaciated gifts gathered from the forest floor.

I always wondered why he didn't put up something
really significant.
It wasn't until I grew older and came to understand
the context of things
that I realized there was a pride and a prudence in his purpose.
There were neighbors who didn't need to know
when they were on Timber Ranch land.
And there were others
whom we wanted to think
were still on Timber Ranch land.
So I grew up with a need to circumscribe a piece of land.
A piece of land that belonged to me,
land that I found and acquired and began to own.
Therein lies the rub.
The dream has always had that paradoxical moment when we –
he and I –
would stand next to a hole and set that fence post,
that corner post that said, "this is mine."
This is where theirs leaves off and mine begins.
Knowing where we've been and how long it's been since
we stood at the corners,
we also know that as his sons spent time with him
mine spend time with me –
walking the corners.

RED SOCKS

There he was, sloping shoulders,
graying hair, the "monk's spot,"
long, dangling ears and glasses.
Dressed in a gray shirt, blue pants and loafers,
he was just an ordinary man.
But no!
With his back to me in the left aisle, he went through
all of the motions of the church service.
And then he sat down and there they were –
Red Socks!
The whole scene changed.
And I waited and thought of that delightful message.
His choice!
Then he turned, wishing his neighbors well,
and his eyes hinted at the rest of the story.
They were dancing, twinkling waterfalls, sharing love.
And there, accompanying his brilliant acknowledgments,
and hanging low on his long stony jaw
was a gracious smile.
I watched him leave the service,
he sloped to one side and had a slight limp.
Ah, but he had said it all when in the morning
he made his choice!
A splash of joy on an old man's foot.
How did he know I would be there?
Thank you!
And Amen!

LANGUAGE

A tongue,
it continues to expand into the species,
sinking into every corner of the globe,
crossing seas and mountains,
deserts and plains,
forests and jungles
used by a wandering band.
Coalesced by time and circumstance to be
usurped by kings and queens.
Carried by scouts and soldiers,
we find it changing rapidly.
Announcing births, marriages, feasts, or peace,
a relative terminology, always emerging,
carried by nomads, pilgrims, pioneers, or preachers.
It has circumnavigated the globe,
picking up new words here and new phrases there,
a color, a meaning, an object.
Soaking up the facts and lure of the species,
bending to the need of the moment,
opening avenues to understanding.

It changes,
carped at by some, loathed by others.
Embraced in joy or ecstacy by prisoners
as familiar sounds are heard,
and we know that we can share our thoughts and feelings.
All utterances are made with the haste of need
and tarry not in formalities.
As with the heart of the organic,
the paintbrush of God always moves too fast for most of us,
and yet
it does that which there is to do:
Shares being with being.
It communicates.
Humanity unfolds in itself.
The Word speaks.

SOLITARY

She shuffled down the sidewalk,
listing heavily to the left,
practicing the ancient art of balance of the aged.
The eternal "purse" hung from the crook of her left arm.
Where was she going?
How far had she come?
Each crack in the sidewalk a nemesis,
each tilted driveway a potential fall.
She paused to rest,
not too long,
the purpose of the journey must have been important.
Alone,
indomitable,
frail,
committed,
a beauty to behold.
A prayer's purpose –
to acknowledge.
Thank you!

WINDOWS

Yes!
There it is again!
God, how I love the sun's rays!
Vibrant and dynamic they linger, or so it seems,
as they gently and incessantly bathe the world.
Illuminating and obfuscating,
creating shadows and blinding brilliance.
Shadows giving birth to dark hiding spots of soft stillness,
containing temperature differentials that envelop,
and plunge feelings into memories of caves,
savannahs and tundra.
Dazzling light burns our simple apertures,
and we scream, no!
Yet behind that fiery radiance we know something hides,
caught in God's eyes only.
The wind and light,
partners dancing to seasonal rhythms.
Who leads? Does it matter?
An infinite repertoire of movements,
choreographed by the Unseen Hand.
All this gives a fertile reality to the poet's mind's eye.

Yeses and nos,
enchantment draws piqued wonder,
awe builds,
a caldron of feelings boil,
words tumble,
the process is at hand!
The architect said,
"Why so many windows?"
And the carpenter,
"You sure have a lot of glass!"
The environmentalist mused,
"Heat loss? Heat gain?"
All I said was,
"For the soul to see."

NO!

An accident,
the sirens scream,
the crowd assembles,
a few friends stand dumbfounded.
A last hushed breath is taken
in some strange distant place.
Why do they go?
What are they looking for?
Does youth ever know?
I didn't when I went on my journey to the unknown.
What did my parents think?
They never said.
They must have had those pangs of pain,
those that come when we can't understand.
I touched them all – upon occasion.
Will that time spent ever be enough?
It has to be –
that is all we had.
The capriciousness of life
presents itself as some muffled, ancient shuffle.
We hold, we touch, we tickle, and we spank,
the moments fade in memory's soup.
One more time!
That's all I ask.
Did they know that I loved them?
Did I know that they loved me?
Being's mystery is all there is.
Except that call from the heart that says,
"Children, you were mine,
I knew you once."

THE CHAIN SAW

A little thing,
too small to cut the big timber.
Ah, but just right for the artist's hand.
The builder,
the seer of visions,
of cabins and barns
with laughing guests
whose hearts,
free at last,
kneel in silent praise.
Benches and doors,
cabinets and closets,
all nooks and crannies
of some wandering mind.
The exhaust of gas and oil
mixed with the scent of pine
sends a message that something is taking shape.
A nightmare or a dream,
it matters not.
The deed is done and something left behind.
Time spent in making –
that's our purpose.

OCTOBER TIME

You are full, complete,
you have labored long enough.
Color bursts forth and says, "I am done!"
The temperature is crisp and clean.
The scents of summer fade to a finished fall finality.
The coyote's voice has a plaintive ring,
The elk's bugle carries a message of eerie insistence.
Small flocks of weary winged travelers spend fleeting seconds
nurturing courageous hearts for lengthy flights.
The grasses have been burned an appropriate brown.
A soft earthen color beckons and reminds,
from dust to dust …
Does nature waste?
What happens to the cobwebs when summer's work is done?
The time is still,
summer's breezes have all died.
Silence reigns interrupted only by stark blue skies.
Moments are so quiet, the ringing in my head
interrupts my thoughts.
The clouds have all gone home.
Azure broken only by the black wings of ravens.
Our breathing becomes slow and measured,
broken periodically with sighs.
The buzzing of an itinerant fly
and the raukish jay's renderings –
all sounds of things taking care of last-minute details,
before Old Man Winter decorates for the Joyful Season.
The sun's rays drive eyelids to droop.
We, like the rest of creation, seek to rest.

Then suddenly, high in the pines and off in the distance,
a hushed roar of the marauding wind sweeps across the earth,
rising to crescendos and wails.
The message comes –
our days are numbered.
A cool shade comes upon us and we sense the Truth,
summer's dead, yet no tears are shed.
In the final act of honest acceptance, we know
it's true but doesn't matter.
The last butterfly, a yellow one,
vanishes among the many gray heads of the meadow's flowers.
Somehow, as the wind riffles the pages,
we hear the crackling of the parchment of another time,
and yet we know the feelings were and are the same.
As I take one last look into my October Time,
I think this must be God's favorite season.
I catch light flashing low across the meadow,
dipping wings are heading south,
and now I know I too must go.
It hurts to write,
I stop,
the last waning rays of the sun warm my old hands,
the pain is gone – for the moment.
I am reminded, "Can you help them if you don't rest?"
The smell of smoke lingers
into the late afternoon and gentle evening.
The soft silver fluff mixes with the moonlight,
merging into the Indistinct,
becoming a part of the Bridge of Time.
Memories are carried on October's shoulders
into the winter's night.

CHOICES

"Give us the child, you can have another!"
The gang leader shouted,
"We will kill him anyway!"
The mother continued to hold the child.
The brutality of the gang raged.
A young stranger entered the throng.
Quietly he said,
"If you must kill someone,
kill me and let the mother and child live."
The gang members laughed and killed all three,
the young mother,
the child,
and the young stranger.
The gang members chanted,
"There are other children, let's find one!"
Decisions,
choices,
what difference do they make?
There were those gang members who could not forget
scenes from their haunting past.
"Why would the young mother hold so tenaciously
to her child?"
"Why would a young stranger offer himself?"
What choices does life offer?
What choices does life demand?
There are those examples of commitment
that shine forever in time.
Life must be lived
so that in living we make a statement about life.

THE HOWLING

The banquet was set,
a long table,
friends and family,
Knights, Ladies, and children,
roast duck,
roast pork,
roast pheasant,
candied fruit, nuts, cake,
and sherry.
Aromas melted, commingling
with the warmth of the blazing hearth.
Soft music bonded time and soul.
Conversations of work, hunting, and offspring,
to the third generation, flowed freely.
Everyone sharing from full hearts.
With goblets and chalices all filled,
the celebration began.
The old Knight reflected:
His Lady, his children, his friends, his land,
his horses, his dogs,
true fulfillment.
He slowly dipped his finger in his sherry-filled goblet,
gently circling its rim.
His old blue eyes settled on the form of his Lady
as a soft, high-pitched note became
part of the evening's delights.
Amid the clamor and revelry,
an ear tuned through the years heard the lonely note.
Raising her face
she looked into the old Knight's deep blue eyes
and smiled, nodding.

The Lady dipped her finger in her chalice,
slowly and methodically circling its lip,
a higher note joined the evening's lure.
The old Knight lifted his goblet,
and in a silent gesture they toasted each other.
The festivities deepened in texture and tone.
The fireplace was stoked, delicious food filled stomachs,
company fed the spirits,
sherry opened memories' doors,
flames warmed bodies and hearts.
With his goblet half full,
the old Knight smiled at the evening's sharings.
Again dipping his finger into the sherry,
he rhythmically rubbed the rim of his goblet.
A solid, full-bodied note
melted into the din of voices and laughter.
Turning, the Lady listened and smiled
and caught the old Knight's subtle grin.
Delicately she dipped her finger in her half-filled chalice,
moving her hand about its lip she sent an answer back to him.
He raised his goblet as she raised hers,
"A toast," he said.
The joyful conversation and laughter ceased.
He stood and simply said,
"To the bounty of life!"
His head moved as his eyes caught momentarily
those of each guest.
They were good friends, neighbors all.
They labored in the administration of their land.

Men and women who would work shoulder to shoulder
with anyone at any task,
never too menial, never too small,
always generous and more than willing to help each other.
His eyes completed the circuit of the assemblage,
finally, resting gently upon his Lady, he added,
"And to the ladies, the greatest boon to every man!"
"Here! Here!"
all intoned with great enthusiasm,
turning towards their respective mates,
embraces and kisses telling stories
of the eternal depth of life.
The old Knight's eyes fixed upon his Lady's gaze.
Locked together, they bridged time immemorial,
exchanging mutual admiration and devotion.
They shared life's full basket.
The evening's activity slowed,
wine and food calmed joyful hearts and bodies.
The celebration was a needed respite
from the labors of the seasons.
Heartfelt "Thank yous" were shared all around.
The guests, gathering their own,
retired to journey homeward.
Children and grandchildren all hugged the Knight and the
Lady.
Laughing and full of life's zest,
they shared their living with impatience and sincerity.
At last the Knight and the Lady stood alone,
arm in arm,
surveying the scattered remnants of the occasion.
He took his goblet and finding a few drops,
dipped his finger to the very bottom.

Once again he stroked the rim.
A deep-throated note resembling a howl flowed forth.
Vibrations filled the great room.
Smiling deeply the lady dipped her finger
to the very bottom of her near empty chalice,
gently circling its lip.
A low-pitched feminine echo joined the enveloping vibrations.
A knowing gaze spoke of years,
struggle and pain,
joy and ecstacy,
all courses in life's full meal.
Turning with hands entwined
they mounted the stairwell to their lair,
raspberries, music, libations, family and friends,
simply not quite enough of a dessert for the banquet of life.
Soulmates who understood the depth of sharing,
knew well the simple fare that nourished love.
Murmurings merged with the fading notes' echoes.
Embers glowed with their last dazzling light.
The moon's rising bathed the snow-clad world.
A gift of life was shared.

THE BOX

There was the yellow notice:
"Too large for the P.O. box."
What great thing was it?
Who had bothered to send a "big" thing?
With anxious heart I waited.
The Postmaster said, "Here it is."
Yes!
I knew who it was from,
A Christmas package from Lucerne!
A brown bulging cardboard box,
plastic tape and old markings,
nondescript – except for the mystery hidden within.
Hoping that "the wrapper" *this time* had done their duty,
I hurried home,
wondering what strange, old thing
or tasty delight
was tucked away.
And Yes!
And yes again!
There they were, each and every treasure,
cookies I had not seen for decades and more –
dark, rich molasses, and filled!
Soft, white decorated *real* Christmas Cookies!

And the little "pies" with corrugated edges!
Will there always be a mother somewhere
who will take the time to love the task?
And wait!
What heavy object lies below?
Behold – the golden color.
Behold – the nectar of the maple.
Memories again spill forth.
Dripping spring days and pails,
slush, wet boots, cold fingers, and the smell of smoke!
Will there always be memories to stir the soul –
I mean in Heaven, too?

A FATHER, A BROTHER, MY FELLOW MEN

Life is for doing!
Great tasks burn in our hearts.
How and when will we be able to lift the logs to resting places
without our fathers, our brothers, and our fellow men?
How is it that we can leave our hallowed homes,
cross rivers and mountains in search of the proper place,
that sacred ground?
And when we do – we are left alone,
no fathers, no brothers, no fellow men
to stand shoulders bent,
all making mutual gifts of presence.
Can we bridge this hollow, empty silence,
a place where no heavy breathing hangs in the crisp fall air?
The deeds stay the same.
Dreams are made of eternal stuff.
But when we are left alone,
how can we lift logs to resting places?
The fire burns.
The wind blows.
The coyote howls.
And somewhere in the hidden recesses of our hearts,
memories rise up and say,
"It is not for us to know why we are here alone."
All that matters is
that our fathers, our brothers,
and our fellow men believe.
With this we lift the logs to resting places.
We move great mounds of earth.
Stones are laid to form the altar.
The deed is done!

CONVOCATIONS

There will come a time when
relegated to the edges, we will see new hearts grow.
For now,
we are the center,
we must give them all we have.
I say to my mate,
"Stay with me so that we will know when the moment comes
to let *new life* take the stage."
She nods a gentle yes.
To each a season with its time,
a touching producing life.
Forming links in the eternal chain of God's Great Work,
families are born.
A Great Table must be built.
Celebrations will come quickly.
A Great Hall to hold them all will ring with life
when convocations are at hand.
Long poles must be set.
Flags must be flown.
Heraldry must be invoked.
Trumpets must be blown.
There will be children running and laughing
with peals of delight echoing across meadows.

All of this and much more
will give great pleasure and meaning to our gatherings.
Yet the time will come
when the elderly will sit quietly at one side.
Scales will be tipped by a critical mass of youth.
The next generation will be looking towards new horizons.
Nodding patiently, we will stand aside.
Smiles will cross our faces.
Knowing glances will be shared.
The changing of the guard will be at hand.

SPRING SCENE

Next to a fence
stands a young man
gazing at a horse.
Seeking, stroking hands fall.
Magnificent arched neck drops.
A soft muzzle floats over new-green meadow grass.
In pastels of spring
majestic forms of promise
share power and presence.
Scenes come, causing wonder to fly vanquished
when we know we've caught a glimpse of
dreams entering souls' windows.

MOLASSES COOKIES

Mounds of freshly piled earthen dough
all covered with a dusting of snow.
What pregnant possibilities!
Crushed cane,
a season's crispness,
accents with pungent delight.
Soft, brown circles touched by thick, dark syrup,
sprinkled with sugar or iced,
are gifts
for soft, slippery mastication
and much rumination.
Simple cookies,
they warm hearts
and tease reason.

THE GATHERING

The occasion,
to see a dear friend off,
others – a Commencement.
Life's new chapters to be written,
from the youngest to the oldest
they gathered.
Libations and morsels were shared by all.
The festive spirit reigned.

* * *

Too often life's chores steal
by cluttering our time.
Hours spent with friends are long forgotten.
Then – a celebration comes and we remember.
Familiar faces, hugs and handshakes are met with
bright, expectant eyes acknowledging presences.
Twinkling, moist, they say,
"Welcome!"
A warmth of belonging fills the air.
The chatter for the celebration fades
and catch-up-talk of where and when we've been
takes the floor.
New additions to the circle are brought in.
A settled hum of conversation spiked with laughter
pervades the moments.

Bowed and nodding heads,
swaying from face to face giving gracious sustenance,
are proof of the depth of friendship.
Melting hearts are freed from the world's cares.
Children pass from group to group
tugging at fingers, skirts, and trousers,
listening in two languages.
A child held and touched by everyone stares wide-eyed
full of awe.
The Truth says,
"This is what life is all about!"
And then, with the suggestion of music, he rises.
Stiffly his legs move towards the guitar.
His hands gently take the instrument.
Long years of intimate relationship tell the tale.
Smiling, he sits.
His stiff left leg offers support
as nimble fingers touch notes to life drawn from fading years.
He takes center stage,
age a meaningless fact,
as familiar lyrics tumble from cobwebbed minds.
The assembly remembers melodies and phrases,
sheer joy of sharing blurs perfection.
Requests come from all sides.
Heroic attempts are made
to place notes and words in proper places.
Choices are a yes and no as they hurry on.
Drinking deep from sharing's need,
souls sing.

JUST MOMENTS

The hawk,
a fleeting form
reflected in a chipmunk's eye.
For a weasel,
death
a daily event.
Sap's flow ceasing,
abscission layers form.
Leaves fall.
Frozen crystals melt.
Liquid moves.
Rhizomes seek.
Lightning flashes.
Souls' heartbeats skip.
Thunder comes.
Full wombs.
Life spills.
Children cry.

HANDLES

The sweep in the handle of an axe.
Torn blisters turned to calluses.
Centuries of blade meeting trunk and limb.
What arc?
What plane?
Who knows how it is that discoveries are made
that set thoughts to tasks?
Subtle angles in our tools
wrought from efforts of the ages
are gifts telling tales of triumphs.
Intrepid laborers,
inventive geniuses,
from we who hold the hammer, saw, auger, adz and axe,
our deepest gratitude.

THE ALBUM

Thick leather covers bind large black pages
covered with winding trails of life's effort.
Square little histories of the species' convolutions,
where threads of mitochondria mix with global geography –
all pieces of our family,
form a small mosaic.
Fading photographs in rows
are gently turned.
Years fall away as we see a canoe gliding along Nordic shores,
trips to Jolly Old England and to the Ranch,
festivities capturing weddings, births, accomplishments,
holidays, and gatherings.
Where has the time gone?
How much do they,
or we, remember?
"Too little,"
the fear says,
as memory's musty veil is lifted higher and higher.
Smiles, frowns, and candor
present a flow of life's expressions.
"When was this?
Who is that? Oh look!
Yes! Yes! And yes again!"

Those gracious gifts called children
begin on horizontal planes.
Then shoot by us on the rise
as soft features condense in character and deeds.
The lineage's apogee reached,
lauded, and lost.
How often do we sit and sense
those humbling times
when fingers turn years
to seconds,
touching
the lost and the missing?
Efforts crushed by time
start to crumble.
Parent's dreams and aspirations for self and others,
some drawn out,
become moments of shimmering light and shadow,
blurring in history's huff.
Their turn now
as empty pages wait.

EQUUS

Majestic heads,
driving withers,
thrusting haunches,
pounding hooves,
you come charging across history's pages.
Your strong hearts and heaving sides
were harnessed to carts, wagons, chariots and caissons.
You came pulling cargos of plunder and slaves,
shot and powder,
pioneers and hope.
You walked ahead of graceful carriages,
plodded in wagon trains,
raced before the spear,
plowed fertile valleys,
nuzzled meadow grass
with children resting on your broad backs.
You, with ears set to the master's call
and the season's message,
reaped harvests of labor and love,
traversed wide avenues of great civilizations,
hauled over continental divides and plains.
Your work was all done with an integrity of task.
You stepped forever forward, dripping sweat,
with no thought to history's chapters.
I miss your staying presence,
your ponderous strength and soft, gentle muzzle.

QUILT

Of the many blessings come to me,
it must be easy for all to see –
for one I am most grateful.
In morns crisp I tug and pull
tiny feathers encased in tight-stitched cloth
as I dreamily await a scenting of the broth.
My goose's labors lost
guard me from the frost ...

THE BATON

It moves,
a tiny thing of great proportions.
Subtle in its grandeur,
arcing, pointing,
staying even,
in search of coincidence.
How does a composer
gather notes and scales
mounting to heights
above the soul's vision,
or slipping to depths
below the roots of the heart?
Crescendos send crashing waves through senses' ports.
Movement forms a lattice connecting each player
to an instrument and to self.
Size and shape, color and substance,
fit bound by the eternity of compatibility,
discrimination an anathema to their purpose.
Sounds now racing, then plodding,
circling and separating,
bursting to coalesce.
All
belonging to
the Great Movement …
Is there some hand
that catches droplets of foam
from the crests of all the oceans' waves
and gives them to a Master's Mind
who sets them to a score?

Does a singular eye penetrate the mists and shadows
of deep, dense, tangled swamps and forests
in search of emotions' paths
that through notes
send vibrations
to windows, doors, vents, drains and chimneys of the soul?
From pinnacles of windswept, snow-covered, craggy peaks,
shoulders break away to broad tumbling torsos and
verdant inclines with silver lacing cascades' rainbows
giving birth to dawns drowned in fog.
The Master's heart collects sharps and flats for banquets,
sending guests beyond any range of comprehension.
As we float awash in a personal reverie
that cements us to ourselves,
on tongue, held by soft lips and clenched teeth, rolling, lifting,
stopping, jerking, waving,
the baton maintains its appointed purpose:
Pulling from the hidden depths of practiced hours
a faithful rendition
of the Master's Sojourn.
With souls lifted, amid awe and rolling tears of joy,
pins are pulled to turn the pallet.
He rotates slowly
towards his audience
and with a delicate nod of his maned head
the conductor takes his bow.

HISTORY'S HILL

For those who are left and those who turn
to see the view from history's hill,
all our yesterdays lie below.
The smoke drifts,
we stand awestruck for that final look back.
The ground is stained,
the bodies lay,
the battle is over.
History in bits and pieces of human flesh,
torn from children,
from women,
and from men.
Values died for,
families destroyed,
friends lost,
homes left in ashes.
As we stumble up the hill and turn,
we see
the scorched earth,
the rubble,
the simple and the profound,
all scattered in the winds of time.
All forever rising,
forever falling,
something always becoming something else.
A purpose to it all?
Says the Voice,
"Just keep heading up the hill."

WOLFER

I hear your plaintive cry,
or is it mine I hear?
I think I see you
and feel your presence.
Wolf – your silent shadow slips through evening times
when soft, gentle breezes wane
and you are lit by the hazy moonlight
sifting through pine needles and misty clouds.
Pain and streams of teardrops come and fall.
A mighty longing rips sinew from my bones.
I am left a helpless mass.
Come lay your muzzle in my hands.

THE BAUBLE

A meadow, a homestead, a veteran, a dream,
in '26 he came, labored and loved,
lost and left.
The fence hung on in many places
from broken posts and pines.
Much fell nestling in the ponderosa's dead brown needles.
Till at last horses came from Texas
and forgotten wire was resurrected.
Pulled from tangled branches and set in straight lines
to new peeled posts and notched trees,
its rusted corpse hung once again
in weather fair and foul,
keeping in and keeping out as its maker had intended.
The story goes its birth came early one fall morning,
when stretching twisted ends,
one tore through a glove
and loosed a stream of red.
Trimmed and set to rest
the curled and hooked piece
was left hanging from its newfound place
to bask in singular delight.
Swaying in the breezes
adding its faint squeaking rhythm
to Nature's gentle chorus.
A curiosity for birds
whose cocked heads sometimes peer in wonder
as they perch in the bauble's crook.

ODE TO ADOBE

You rise up as the spade cuts and mounds the surface.
Sifted into a smooth texture with added ashes
you're ready for the stiffness of the straw.
Then, when water finally touches you,
you become slippery mush.
Formed to blocks and left to dry, your journey has begun.
Piled against the earth from which you came
your protective spirit shelters against wind and weather.
The mass of your heart is cool in summer and warm in winter.
To you we owe so much.
We sing in seasons of joy and pain.
Through centuries of service to our kind
we praise your name.

GOD'S SOUL

The grand measure of God's Soul
is that in the coalescence of the universe
His heart beats again
and in this thrown-ness into freedom
choice defines our souls.

BROKEN BRANCH

The storm came and left its calling card.
A broken branch hung dangling in the wind.
Then it fell –
embracing its beginning.

BACCHUS

What say thee to hours lost in swill?
Are there those whose wanderings
crossed same's threshold?
As said before, it matters not,
the gift is choice,
not labors bound to bend thy knee.
Freedom reigns supreme!
Moments with the gifts of love are wine.
Whose bouquet brings depth to harvests
wrought from vineyards worlds away?
Touched palettes lose their senses
when imagination reigns supreme!
Time lost.
Deeds undone.
Life's precious light dimming.
Soul's ecstasy spent in wanting.

ON A CRESTFALLEN HILL

The edge endured no more,
it fell into itself.
Melting ignominiously, becoming indistinct,
it sank in weathered form.
Does it matter where we die?
Not in the least,
if we bask in the sun of the Divine.
We must learn the art of waiting.
There is a different cadence in the rhythm of the Eternal
that sends a calming message to us all:
Any place is a good place to die.
We know,
because we've been,
that we are a part of the Whole.
Is there any needed accolade that could add more?
Amen!

CELEBRATIONS

Smoldering candlesticks,
is that all that's left?
Is the end to be in coiling smoke?
What was it for?
Where was I?
I touched them when they were young.
Did they grow away from me or did I abandon them?
Can feelings caught in joy last forever?
The black is here,
insight blurred.
Swiftly sweeping time and the light is lost.
Who's left dancing?
Who's setting souls free?
Are we in the meadow now?
Am I finally with the Lady?
Is the beauty of imperfection still in the flower?
Has life come and gone?
Are we still in His hand?

DIASPORA

The coalescence of the All,
the light from the dark,
the beginning of the birth of God.
As the universe breathes
so does the soul of God express itself.
As we travel forward in time
we touch the face of the Effervescent,
and we all must reach out again and again
and touch and say,
I love you!
I love you!
To each and every thing,
"I love you!"

GLOWING WINDOW

Light in the castle window!
The torrents of time and circumstance
bleed our being.
We must be there.
The gauntlet has been thrown.
We have responded.
Where is our time,
the hearth, the fire, your touch?
The winds howl.
The silence screams.
Agony is frozen in life's forms.
Endless battles
scourging wrong from right.
Tired and hungry.
The road is long.
The light is dim.
Finally,
there upon the hill,
sustained by hope,
the Knight dismounts.
The door swings wide.
The staircase scaled.
At last repose,
her form,
his arms.
The silence of the lost fire in the ashes
speaks of long hours of sharing.
Dawn will come!

GIFTS OF THE FIRE WATCHER

He would sit every evening,
contemplating, as it were,
The Enemy.
Flickering flames curled gently
around carefully cut and split logs.
Summer and fall's commitment
to scrounging less-than-perfect wood,
the cast-offs of the logging industry,
junk stolen from the humus.
It was all kindling for those reflective hours
when the contained oxidation mirrored the truth
and fostered quiet times for conjuring
plans that would be set in motion.
He listened intently to the hiss and snap of moisture and sap
that said,
"Get on with life!"
As he watched the jailed marauder evening after evening,
he followed through on his life plans.
He taught me all I'll ever know
about philosophy and
life's commitments.
Thanks, Dad!

FOCUS

Being and time,
a spontaneity!
Sifting thoughts,
an incremental contribution to eclectic focus,
where movement and light make all the difference.
And,
ah ha, that elusive desire.
A condemnation to eternally see God from behind,
as history is our only fodder.
The radiance enthralls in waning
and yet
there is that burning to see His face in the NOW!
Ever to be done?
Is not that the pull of Hope shrouded in Faith
and beckoned by Charity?
So we move!
To Dasein and to Martin,
Thank you!

THE LAND

To pay for the land –
a piece of steppe, a piece of canyon, a piece of lakeshore,
a piece of flatland, a piece of rock, a piece of sand,
a piece of valley, a piece of forest,
a piece of land.
Some with water, some with trees,
all with blood, sweat, and tears.
What is the cost of the land?
Wandering nomads, chariots of slaves,
kingdoms and continents.
How much does it cost? How much?
The desire blurs the vision and the senses,
and the purpose of life is brought to question.
Why a piece of land?
A primitive urge pounds away at a man's heart and soul
and rends the fabric of the Holy.
And still ...
THE LAND!
The bend of the river, the bottom land,
the broken ground and the sweet smell
of fertile soil and sawdust.
Dreams in drops of sweat.
Time suspended in plans.
Some with water, some with trees.
All with blood, sweat, and tears.
We labor lost in being with an insatiable thirst
for a primitive conquest:
a piece of ground.
And in the end,
at the banquet table,
to taste the dust.

LOONS

Eerie cries echo across plaintive misty mornings
and gentle evenings,
bouncing indirectly from the water to the hills.
Communication's sensuous undertaking
from dark forms spending time slipping beside each other
gently touching,
arched in preening,
subtle in their caring.
A scene set in space far from intrusions
giving a presence just for each other and their progeny.
Gifts adding serenity to God's self-portrait,
basking in the moonlight as it makes small silver dishes
in the gentle waves of silent nights.
Diving and feeding,
shaking and playing,
stately statuettes
lying immobile in time.
Cast in black and silver,
they feed my haunting memories.

THE LESSON

$$MC^2 = E$$
But wait!
Is there something missing?
What about condemnation, or the resurrection of matter?
Time only runs in one direction, doesn't it?
Are we all good and evil in the now?
Just converging being?
A singularity!
So?
In the stillness of a Black Hole,
what voice speaks?
Reciprocity!
Then something is inevitable?
Yes!
But we won't see …!
Perhaps the soul of the universe is pure energy.
Will there be light again?
It may not matter.
And music, will there be the joy of sound?
We won't know.
What then, only the eye and ear of God?
No!
What will there be?
As the Singularity drops through itself …
Yes?

Waves ripple out into the void ...
Waves of what?
Particles!
But nothing can escape, where do they go?
To the center of the Singularity.
And then what?
The summit of the cone becomes ...
Yes? Yes ...?
A spiral helix centered on a vortex turning out
and away from itself in that supreme sacrifice of One.
Ah ha!
And then we have a new beginning?
$E = MC^2$
But isn't that just local physics?
Perhaps.

RED GOLD

The dazzling soft brilliance of the afternoon's lingering light
catches and bathes in His Radiance the grasses and the flowers.
As they dance in the gentle breeze
He plays the waltz,
and they respond with their delicate swaying and bobbing.
The dance is for Him!
To Him they owe their all.
The very forces that flow through them
that they pull from the bowels of the earth,
that they transpire to the heavens,
are prayers to Him.
And the "light" is so that I may see them.
He casts His Love upon them and they dance in His Honor.
In the soft sigh of time
their succor is pulled from His Bosom,
and He takes His Love back to Himself,
as they give themselves to homage Him.
The juices of spring
and the fullness of summer
evaporate gently into fall
and patiently wait through winter.
They were cast and live and die
among the rocks upon the knoll.
They bleed for Thee!
Their sanguine shine is food for me!
Thank You
for giving them to me to see.

SACRIFICE

There is a piece of a starlight's ray or some comet's tail
that came from all of us.
The shared journey was a different point of view
from each perspective:
deprivation from a lover's embrace,
memories from a childhood.
Was the gift of time understood as such?
Not from each was understanding had.
We all view the earth's crucible from vested space.
Happiness and needs are measured by height and weight
and for some in spiritual terms.
We move from wonder and comfort
to awe, food, and a warm bed,
then on to an acceptance of our own truths.
Have we missed the essentials of our time?
Or do we have hidden in the recesses of our hearts
enough of everything?
There were times when hollow spots seemed to be the whole.
I asked God to help me understand
and He gave my me to me.
And so I cry,
"Please show me the Truth of It All!"
I look at a saintly wife and four magnificent children,
and the scene holds answers for the weary mind.
The Truth bubbles forth in a fountain of beauty –
mine to behold,
healthy gifts to the world.

They stand ready to discover their secret formula,
the "Right" solution
to their lives and the world's problems.
Is enough there to serve as a rock of faith that will
guide them through the unknown?
I do believe there is!
The mold was cast from some Celestial Fire,
and we have endured its captivating form.
From sacrifice to gifts
we have made the final leap.
And now,
may we bask in hallowed love for each?

OTHERS

We watch the movie of the world
from our privileged place of serene ignorance,
choosing to disregard humanity's pain and suffering.
How is it that we can still feel "comfortable" with ourselves
and not commit to an incredible responsibility to others?
This was such an essential hallmark of our getting here.
Where has it gone?
Has it disappeared into the numbers of our time?
And if this is so,
why can't we see our neighbors?
What great pile of disregard, or fear, has turned so many
into such blind, uncaring souls?
Does it take a super-abundance of courage
just to love a stranger,
when they come dressed as we
to the party of life?

SHARING

Love is …
two, who upon touching,
give of their inscribed limitations
to explore the possibility of a total and unconditional gift.
A gift of all of one to another,
and in so doing their all to everything.
It is only in this giving of being one that we are set free
to give our gift of freedom.
In the perceived eclectic movement of the universe,
we overcome the limits of our perceptions
and discover a rhythm in which we become a yes to self,
that must in sharing give to another its yesness.
While coincidentally in that sacred crucible of faith,
we become beneficiaries of miraculous reciprocity
as another's yesness is shared with us.
What great tympani of circumstance
gives birth to miracles of life that love?

THE TWENTY-FIRST CENTURY

In the pseudo-sophistication of our time,
we bask in a newfound ignorance.
The cobblestoned streets of history hurt our feet
and the sandals of our leisured life
don't quite serve our current purpose.
We treat the gift of existence with reckless disdain,
knowing full well when we sin.
Still,
we choose other targets for our blame.
Lost in a morassing sea of consumption,
we slake the thirst of our pain with palliatives –
those insidious creations of our boredom.
Who can stand on such a shore,
buffeted by gales of insipid wonder,
without some fleeting recognition of eternal truths
bubbling from our well of being?
Bare those feet
and seek those grains of sand between the rocks,
step into yet another setting sun and beg forgiveness,
lest we abandon the sacred of ourselves.

CEDARS

We make things out of cedar,
the shaggy, soft-barked mascots of the swamps.
Their lower branches, all browsed off by deer,
set the heights of the canopy's bottom –
about six feet between sphagnum and the ceiling of the view –
as if some Gnome Gardener had determined a sacred standard
and pruned them all to size.
There they stood, fragrance held in lacy boughs
with crowns soft shelters for squirrels and birds.
Then came the need for light, soft carvings,
scented, knotty, grained, preserving wood
to house and guard our treasures.
Loggers sought the giants in their sanctuaries,
removing saintly presences from their homes.
Severed trunks laid strung out at trails' ends where skidders
found them and took them to landings
where waiting trucks were
loaded for journeys to whirling saws of commerce.
Thousands of board feet, all ganged to size and shape,
were sent off to mills across the land
for every manner of markets' needs.
We took every piece,
including scraps for arts and crafts.
And so I ask,
Who is planting cedars in the great swamps of our times?

WINDSPEAK

While scaling the peaks and screaming madness
at the world and myself, I tired and fell silent.
My shallow, hot breathing slowed,
beads of sweat were drawn off my brow by a gentle breeze.
Suddenly, I heard a sound, barely audible.
Was it just the wind,
or murmurings,
lost syllables, vowels, dissonance,
sounds of some ancient tongue?
No,
it was voices in conversation.
What is their message?
But wait, I understand them.
A deep belonging fills my soul.
They are speaking as if they know me.
In some way I am connected to them,
intimately familiar.
They are my ancestors!
From some primeval crevasse
the murmurings and shadows come forth.
Silence must be maintained
or they will leave and the message will be lost.
What is it they are saying?

* * *

An assemblage appeared in shimmering, wavering light.
The Matriarch sat facing east to catch the driving rays,
praising the earth,
the birth of each new day,
the children and all things.
The Patriarch sat facing west to catch the waning rays,
pondering where, when, and how.
Speaking as the wind whirled about the peaks
they sat staring into the future,
uttering words,
shrouded in the warmth of their robes.
She said, "Ela, Ela, una y quay!"
Daughters, daughters, the moon lights the way!
He said, "Eluo, Eluo, una y quay!"
Sons, sons, the moon lights the way!
Climb the mountain!
Make the journey!
Learn to see!
Remember,
it is not the view from the mountaintop –
it is the Path that leads you to yourself.

* * *

The children listened and then the children said,
"To climb the craggy peaks at night is dangerous!"
Yes, but it is the only time we can go.
"Why do we have to go at night?"

* * *

The Elders spoke to the children:
"Because you can see more clearly when you must believe.
Confront the shadows of your fears!
The moon's soft light will come from above the racing clouds,
giving you glimpses of
the Path."
The grandfathers and the grandmothers spoke to the parents:
"As we hand you your copy of the ancient parchment,
learn the Rules.
Spend years mastering them.
Prepare a copy for your children's children."

* * *

What is the smudge under each rule?
There must have been something written just beneath each line.
It has been lost over the ages.
Only the deep, dark, large print remains.

PLAY ONE!

STAND STILL IN SILENCE!

TRUE/NOT TRUE — MINE/NOT MINE!

OWN IT NOW!

ACT IN LOVE!

DEDICATE YOURSELF TO GROWTH!

FOLLOW ALL OF THE RULES!

* * *

And the parents spoke to the Elders:
"Tell us again, why must we give the Rules
to our grandchildren?"
The Elders answered:
"Because there is an in-between time
when everyone is too busy to be honest with themselves.
We have been able only to touch the children
and teach the parents
before and after this busy time."
Pangs of guilt drove home the Truth
and the parents shouted,
"But we want to give the Rules to our sons now!
We want to give the Rules to our daughters now!
We will start sharing the Rules when they are very young,
and when they get lost in their adolescence
we will take them to the mountaintop.
We will read the Rules to them.
We will discuss how to use them every day.
We will play the Game of Life together."

* * *

The parents spoke to their children:
"First we will play and then you will play.
We will practice the Rules together.
You will ask, 'Why, Mommy, why?'
You will ask, 'Why, Daddy, why?'
We must explain the unexplainable.
We must tell you where the red goes when the fire burns,
where the white goes when the snow melts.
You must have a reason for doing, for being,
the Truth.

Why else should you learn to love it so?
From time immemorial there have been those
special people,
saints and sages laboring in the sharing of
the Word."
The children asked,
"Where did the Word come from?"
It was in the beginning and in the beginning was
the Word.
"How did anyone learn to understand it?"
It has always spoken to our hearts, our souls,
our bodies, and our minds.
The children asked,
"Why do the Rules work?
What grand design do they represent?
There must be some fundamental logic behind them.
What is it?"
The Elders answered:
"From a line on the ancient parchment we remember,
Who should I say Thou art?"
"I am who I am."
The children shrieked, "That is it!
The Rules are predicated upon that which is what it is,
The Truth of One Now!"
And the smudging on the parchment cleared.
The children said, "Look! Come and see!"

* * *

PLAY ONE!
I must be selfish and honest with myself.

STAND STILL IN SILENCE!
I must be still, alone, to see the Truth of One.

TRUE/NOT TRUE — MINE/NOT MINE!
I must separate the one of the self into my self
and from all others.

OWN IT NOW!
I must do my real Truth of One Now.

ACT IN LOVE!
I must seek self-knowledge, self-care, self-responsibility
and self-respect.
These will light compassion's fire
and connect my self to my self,
and me to my circumstance.

DEDICATE YOURSELF TO GROWTH!
All things move.
I must move according to my own kind.

FOLLOW ALL OF THE RULES!
I can play only one.
As I move in my now towards the Truth of One,
I begin a holy endeavor.

* * *

The parents and children shouted,
"Yes! Yes! They all fit!
The Grand Design, the Folds of Nature, the Soul of God,
'It' is all there!"
"But we never see souls."
The Elders spoke:
"They come alive in moments of desire.
Have you never desired anything
with your whole heart, your whole mind,
your whole body?"
The children answered, "Yes, many times."
"And how did you feel?"
"Consumed!"
"Then your soul is a very strong thing, is it not?"
"Yes, yes it is!"
The Elders added,
"We must follow the rhythm of all life.
Living must be a time of being
One in the Now!
A time of sharing
One Now.
A time of walking with the wind,
singing, dancing, sharing bread,
and making tools,
Now."

* * *

The tired little girls, shivering in the wind,
were wrapped into the robes of their fathers
as they sat looking at
the Truth of One in the Now.
And they said, "We will remember."
The tired little boys, shivering in the wind,
were wrapped into the robes of their mothers
as they sat looking at
the Truth of One in the Now.
And they said, "We will remember."
The moon smiled as it danced over the hills,
hiding and peeking from behind the white gray-black softness.
And the racing clouds laughed among themselves
as silver light was shed upon
The Path.